PreTime® Piano

Jazz & Blues

Primer Level

Beginning Reading

Written and arranged by

Nancy and Randall Faber

Production: Frank and Gail Hackinson

Production Coordinator: Marilyn Cole

Music Editor: Edwin McLean

Cover and Illustrations: Terpstra Design, San Francisco

Engraving: Music Craft of Hollywood, Inc. (Fla.)

Printer: Tempo Music Press, Inc.

THE
F·J·H
MUSIC
COMPANY
INC.

2525 Davie Road, Suite 360
Fort Lauderdale, Florida 33317-7424

A NOTE TO TEACHERS

PreTime® Piano Jazz & Blues is a set of entertaining pieces in a jazz/blues style written especially for children. Traditionally, much of the jazz and blues idiom has expressed life's ups and downs. In keeping with this tradition, **PreTime® Piano Jazz & Blues** includes imaginative lyrics which convey the spirit of jazz and blues to the early grade student. Selections such as *Hound Dog Blues, Dinosaur Stomp,* and *King of Hearts* are sure to please.

The music remains in Middle C Position with an occasional sharp or flat. No eighth notes or dotted rhythms are used, allowing the student to concentrate on a steady beat.

The teacher duets are highly recommended to be used with the student. They not only help the student feel a strong pulse, but also give a real jazz-blues flavor with the expanded harmonies. Delightful illustrations and use of color add excitement to this book. Enjoy opening the door to the sounds of jazz and blues with this immensely appealing *PreTime®* book!

PreTime® Piano Jazz & Blues is part of the *PreTime® Piano* series. "PreTime" designates the primer level of the *PreTime® to BigTime® Piano Supplementary Library* arranged by Faber and Faber. Students may use several *PreTime®* books or graduate to *PlayTime® Piano* (Level 1).

Following are the levels of the supplementary library which lead from *PreTime®* to *BigTime®*.

PreTime® Piano	(Primer Level)
PlayTime® Piano	(Level 1)
ShowTime® Piano	(Level 2A)
ChordTime® Piano	(Level 2B)
FunTime® Piano	(Level 3A–3B)
BigTime® Piano	(Level 4)

Each level offers books in a variety of styles, making it possible for the teacher to offer stimulating material for every student. For a complimentary detailed listing, write the publisher listed below.

Teacher Duets

Optional teacher duets are a valuable feature of the *PreTime® Piano* series. Although the arrangements stand complete on their own, the duets provide a fullness of harmony and rhythmic vitality. And not incidentally, they offer the opportunity for parent and student to play together.

Helpful Hints:

1. The student should know his part thoroughly before the teacher duet is used. Accurate rhythm is especially important.

2. Rehearsal numbers are provided to give the student and teacher starting places.

3. The teacher may wish to count softly a measure aloud before beginning, as this will help the ensemble.

ISBN 0-929666-49-6

TABLE OF CONTENTS

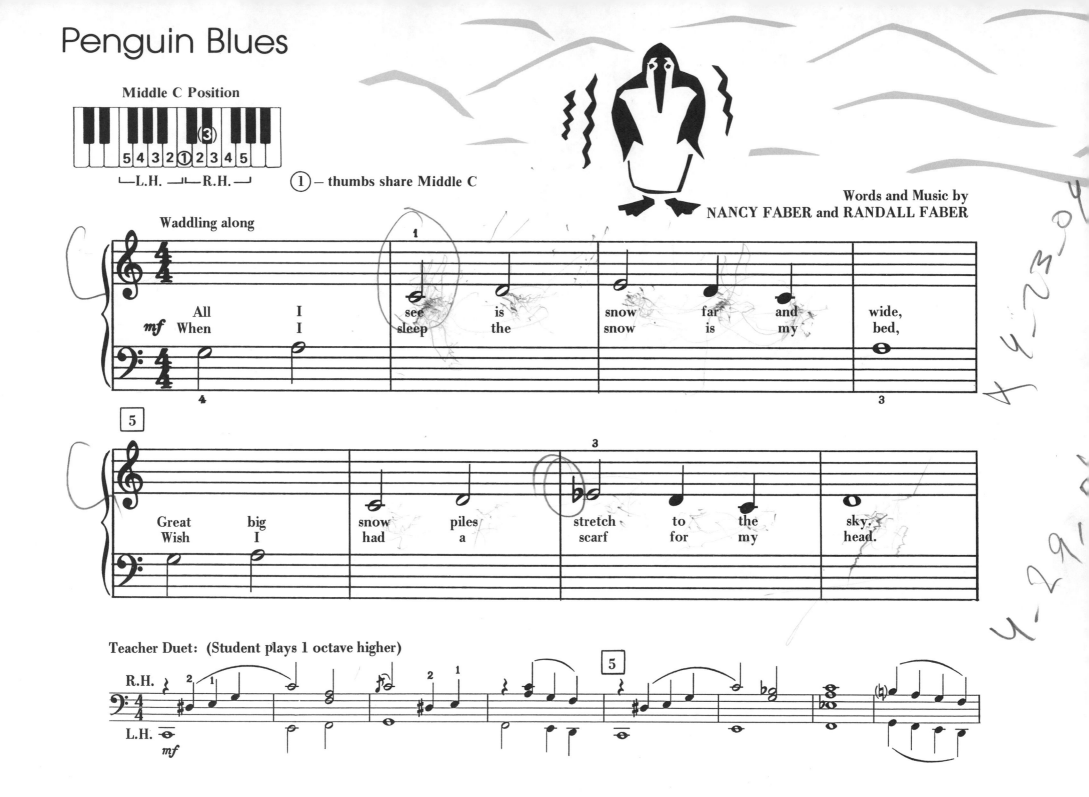

Jazz Walk

Middle C Position

By NANCY FABER

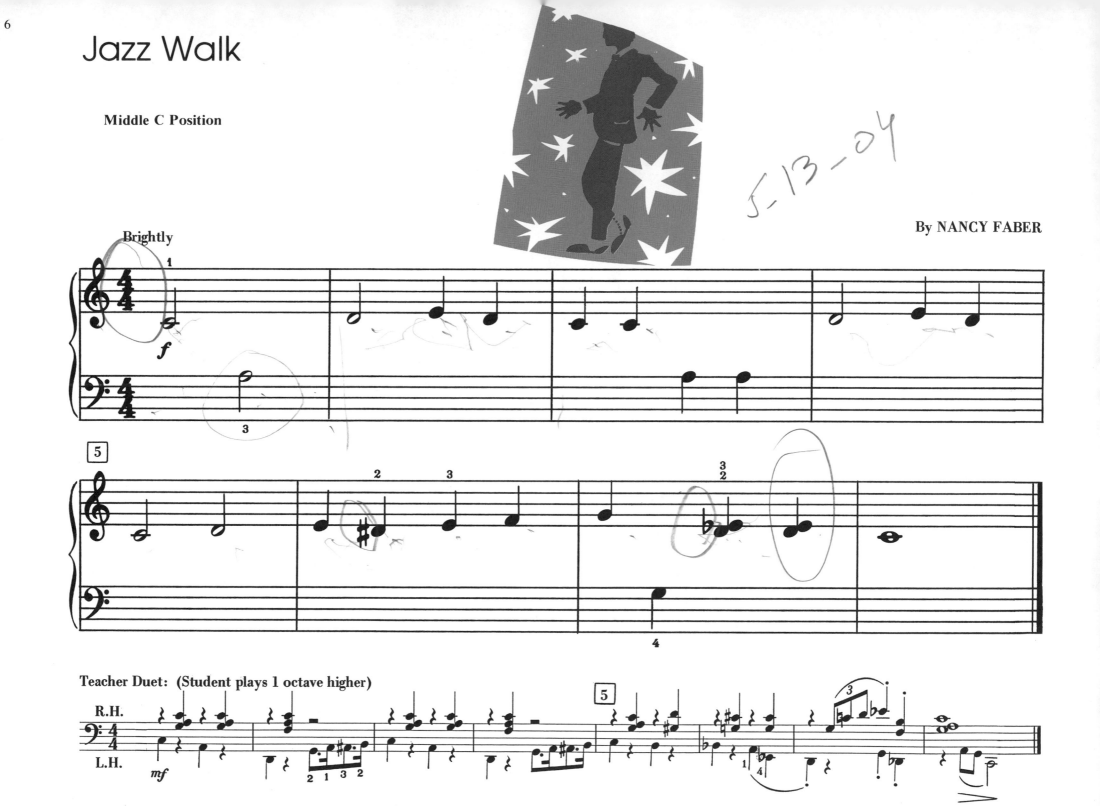

Teacher Duet: (Student plays 1 octave higher)

Hound Dog Blues

Middle C Position

Lyric by **CRYSTAL BOWMAN**

Music by **NANCY FABER**

With big sad eyes

I tore up the pa - per, I chewed on some shoes.

Now I'm in the dog - house, and I'm sing - in' the blues.

Teacher Duet: (Student plays 1 octave higher)

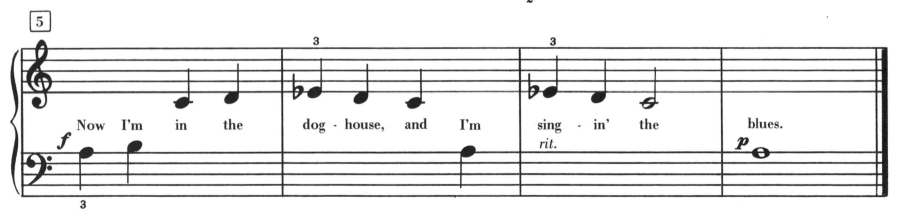

FF1047

Jazz Man

Lyric by CRYSTAL BOWMAN

Music by NANCY FABER

With energy

He picks up his horn _____ an - y time of the day. _____ He can

play an - y tune _____ that you ask him to play. _____ He's

Teacher Duet: (Student plays 1 octave higher)

R.H.

L.H.

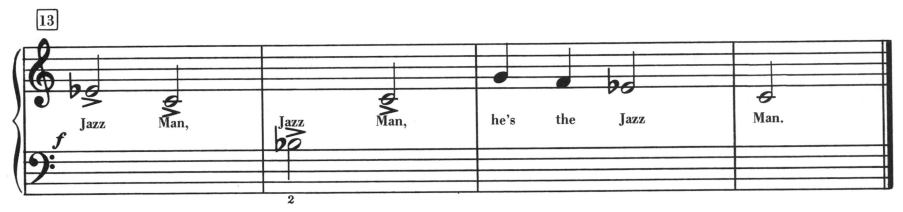

So Many Toys
(So Little Time to Play)

Middle C Position

Lyric by JENNIFER MacLEAN

Music by NANCY FABER

Moving slowly

mf

So man-y toys, so lit-tle time to play.

I wish that bed-time would go far a-way.

Teacher Duet: (Student plays 1 octave higher)

R.H.

L.H.

mp with pedal

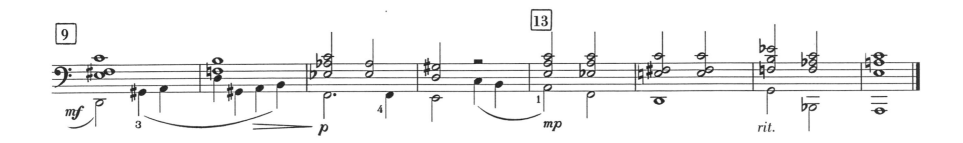

A Fishy Story

Lyric by CRYSTAL BOWMAN

Music by NANCY FABER

Lyrics:
I've been sit-tin' on the dock with my fish-in' pole,
Have-n't caught a fish all day at my fish-in' hole.

Teacher Duet: (Student plays 1 octave higher)

Got a nib - ble and a bite, reeled 'em in with all my might.

But those fish - es ate my bait and swam a - way.

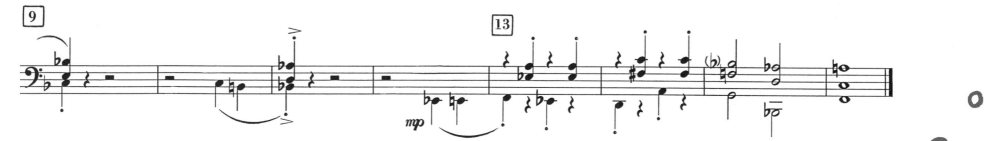

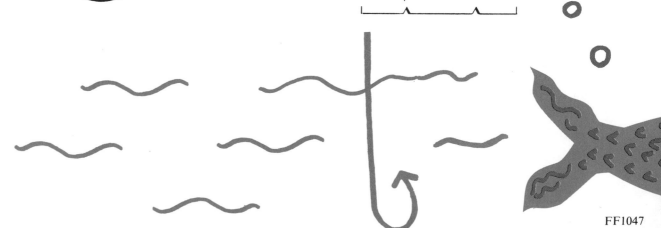

FF1047

Dinosaur Stomp

Words and Music by
NANCY FABER

Crashing along

Crash! Boom! Thunk! Make way, Crash! Boom! Thunk! Love to

roar and do my pre-his-tor-ic danc-in'. All the

Teacher Duet: (Student plays as written)

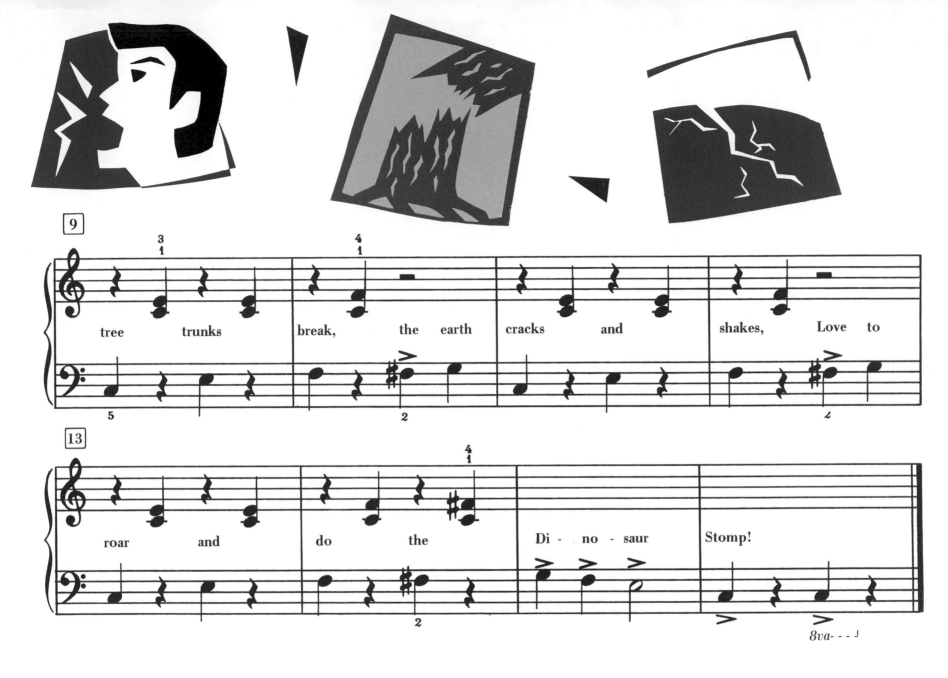

Cool Breeze Waltz

Like a soft breeze

By NANCY FABER and RANDALL FABER

Teacher Duet: (Student plays 1 octave higher)

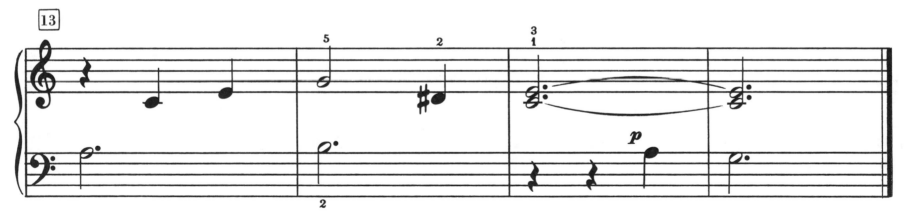

Ice Cream Blues

Lyric by **CRYSTAL BOWMAN**

Music by **NANCY FABER**

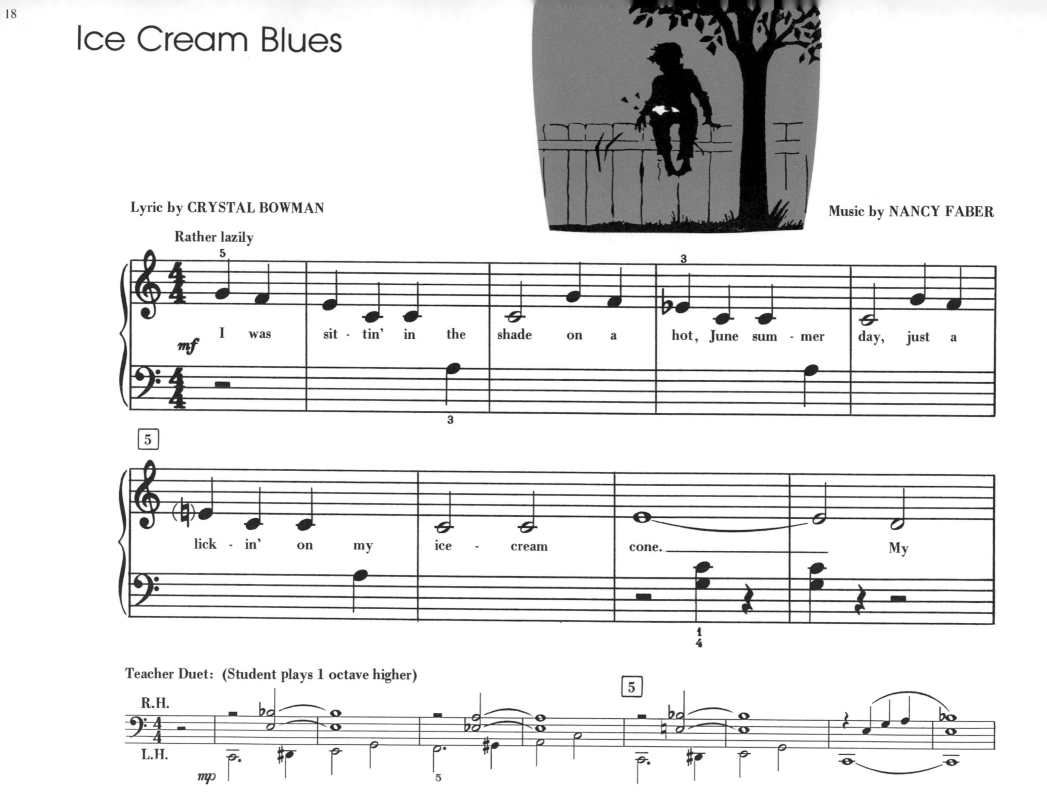

Rather lazily

mf I was sit - tin' in the shade on a hot, June sum - mer day, just a

lick - in' on my ice - cream cone. _____ My

Teacher Duet: (Student plays 1 octave higher)

R.H.

mp

L.H.

The King of Hearts

By NANCY FABER

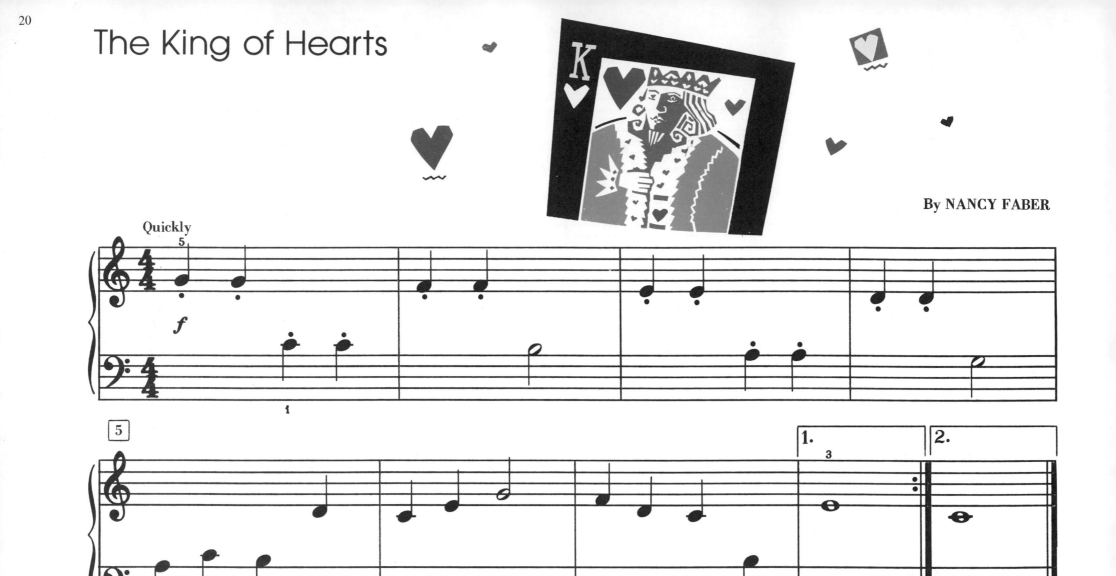

Teacher Duet: (Student plays 1 octave higher)

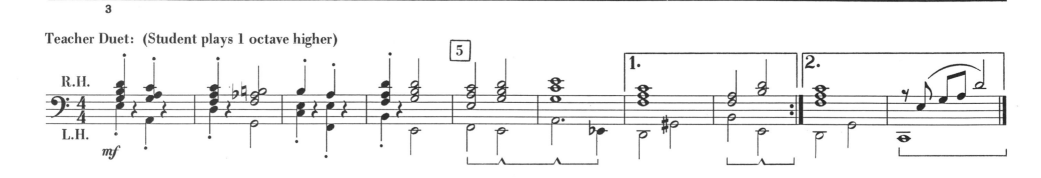